CRISIS IN
LEADERSHIP

"Nothing that you have not given away will ever be really yours. . . . Look for yourself, and you will find in the long run only hatred, loneliness, despair, rage, ruin, and decay. But look for Christ and you will find Him, and with Him everything else thrown in."

—C.S. Lewis[1]

CRISIS IN
LEADERSHIP

K.P. Yohannan

BOOKS

a division of Gospel for Asia

www.gfa.org

ISBN 978-1-59589-116-7

Published by gfa books, a division of Gospel for Asia
1800 Golden Trail Court, Carrollton, TX 75010 USA
phone: (972) 300-7777
fax: (972) 300-7778

Printed in the United States of America

For information about other materials, visit our website:
www.gfa.org.

12 13 14 15 16 17 18 Y/I 7 6 5 4 3 2 1

Table of Contents

Introduction

As leaders, we all want to succeed. We want to build something that will outlast our own lives. But as long as we're human, there can be this nagging fear that we are failing or will fail as leaders. In our efforts to protect ourselves, we often make things worse for ourselves.

This is the crisis we face in leadership today—leaders who feel insecure and threatened in their positions. If insecurity is left unchecked, new leaders aren't raised up and the full potential of many individuals is stifled.

It is my prayer as you walk through this booklet that the Lord will help you to see and recognize the symptoms of insecurity before they become damaging.

May the Lord give us the grace to run the race in His honor.

CHAPTER ONE

A Growing Crisis

Saul was the first king of Israel. He was appointed for a huge task. He was gifted and able. Above all, he was humble, as all God's leaders should be.

Then something went terribly wrong.

Saul started to think he was important and the answer to everything and everyone. He looked strong on the outside, but when trials came, he acted out of fear. Despite his failures, Saul worked hard to maintain a good image with those who served with him.

Then a talented young man under his leadership started to develop—a young sheep herder named David. He was able to defeat the giant and the Philistines, something

Saul was not able to do. David excelled in everything he put his hand to, for which he received high praises from the people.

David was the model of loyalty, but Saul saw him as a threat instead of a blessing from God.

So Saul began making deliberate plans to destroy David. He made accusations, questioned motives and set traps. Saul used every weapon in his arsenal to remove the one he saw as a threat.

Soon people had to walk on eggshells around Saul, knowing that anyone he suspected of being against him suffered terrible consequences.

The sad reality is that he had allowed insecurity to consume his life.

In the end, Saul destroyed his life and the lives of countless men under his leadership.*

The Crisis Today

Which of us, if we were Saul, would not have been at least a little tempted to be jealous of David's increasing success?

Saul was a man chosen by God who allowed jealousy and insecurity to make a shipwreck of his life. His reckless pursuit of

---

* If you have not read it recently, I recommend you read the account of Saul's life as found in 1 Samuel 9–31.

David left Israel for years without a king who was focused on the nation's well-being.

As leaders, it is our responsibility to create an environment in which others can be empowered to excel.

Although it is not frequent that someone is as insecure as Saul was, his life serves as a warning for us of the ultimate devastation insecurity can bring if we allow it to rule our lives.

As leaders, it is our responsibility to create an environment in which others can be empowered to excel. This way, more godly leaders can be raised up and the work of the Lord can go forward.

But when people in leadership positions feel threatened, they can actually hold the kingdom's work back. Their insecurity creates a caustic environment for the people of today and a lack of godly leaders for the people of tomorrow.

During the course of my 40-plus years in Christian leadership, I have witnessed many innocent lives ruined because those in authority felt threatened by the people around them. Like Saul, they are headed for a tragic end. Unless we are able to recognize and deal with this threat when it comes up, it will continue breeding damage in the work of the Lord.

Threatened Leadership

So what do we mean when we talk about leaders being threatened and insecure?

Insecure means "not confident or sure."[1] And *threatened* is defined as "having an uncertain chance of continued survival."[2] When you're insecure you don't feel safe; you just don't know if you can make it where you're at. Being threatened is similar, but it has an added element—a fear that something, or someone, is lessening your chances of survival.

Without the transforming work of the Holy Spirit in our lives, we fight for our reputation, position, respect and ultimately for approval.

When someone feels threatened, they can become like a man who is drowning. In his panic, the struggler becomes quite irrational and frantic in his actions, grabbing anything and doing whatever he can to keep afloat.

Like Saul, people can even become aggressive when they feel threatened, regardless if the threat is real or imaginary. Even a gentle animal when it feels it is in danger can sud-

denly launch a vicious attack. This is basic
animal instinct.

Our natural instinct without the transforming work of the Holy Spirit in our lives
is to *fight* for our reputation, position, respect
and ultimately for approval. As followers of
Christ, we should not be marked by such
striving.

It Happens to Us All

We have all seen brothers and sisters start-
ing off bursting with faith and zeal, willing to
do anything and go anywhere to further the
kingdom. Everything seems to be going well.
But as time passes, their demeanor starts to
change; they become more political in their
orientation rather than spiritual, more inter-
ested in planning and scheming rather than
praying and fasting.

Just like Saul, someone can be called by
God, be empowered and filled by the Holy
Spirit, experience favor in his life and be sur-
rounded by people who support him, yet still
feel insecure.

When I was young, I suffered abuse and
pain under a threatened leader. I continue to
encounter people suffering today, both leaders and the ones who work with them.

It's usually not something we easily recognize in ourselves or a weakness we want to

admit. But this is a problem affecting count-less godly leaders around the world—teach-ers, pastors, deacons, evangelists and mission workers included.

There is an element of insecurity in all of us.

You may be in a position of leadership now or you may end up in one later, but really everyone is responsible for someone or something—*you are a leader*. And you must know there is an element of insecurity in all of us.

There is a temptation, as we read about a topic like this, to look for faults and sins in the lives of those around us. Refrain from that temptation. Instead, ask the Lord to help you approach the next few chapters with an open heart to see whatever He would like to show you for your own life.

May the Lord grant us all the grace need-ed to press on for His glory.

CHAPTER TWO

Symptoms of Insecurity

The first step in nursing an injury is learning to recognize the symptoms. If we don't, we can wind up putting bandages on for a fever or taking medication for a headache when our leg is bleeding.

In the same way, it is important for us to discover how insecurity manifests itself so we can properly "diagnose" it in our own lives.

Not everyone who feels threatened will look exactly the same on the outside, and many of the symptoms of insecurity are subtle and tend to be things we overlook or excuse. But if we can begin to recognize the symptoms, we will be able to address it properly before it spreads into the lives of others.

Praise Seeking

We all need approval, affirmation and encouragement, but when we are insecure, this becomes an almost overwhelming need. We develop an unhealthy desire for praise, longing for people to say, "You are great! There is no one like you!"

In our drive for affirmation and acceptance, we can work very hard, often putting in extra hours. We become restless and competitive. Unfortunately, it's not just a matter of doing a better job or being more responsible. Our efforts become a way of proving, "I am better; I can do it. I deserve the attention and the acclamation."

We seek to receive praise and are reluctant to give it. Instead of recognizing encouragement as a gift that gives to everyone, it can become difficult to acknowledge the successes of others, especially in public. And if others are praised publicly, we can even feel offended and upset. This is the spirit of Cain who killed his younger brother out of jealousy and anger.

When we feel threatened, we look to the words of others to find a sense of stability. Soon we are worrying more about "What do *people* think of me?" instead of "What does *God* think of me?" This is what happened in the life of King Saul.

Wearing a Mask

Despite the fact that Samuel told Saul that God was going to take the kingdom from him for his disobedience, King Saul wanted Samuel to go with him so the people would *think* he was still in good standing with the Lord (see 1 Samuel 15:23–30). In the same way when we feel insecure, the pressing thought is keeping up a good face and looking like we have everything in order.

It can become more important . . .

- to seem to have a godly life than to actually have one

- to appear deeply appreciated by our colleagues than to actually be appreciated

- to seem loving, compassionate and caring than to actually be loving and caring

- to look like we have a godly family instead of actually having one

- to seem smart and intelligent than to actually pursue wisdom

- to look like a "team player" than to actually give value to the opinions and views of others

- to appear loyal to the organization than to actually be loyal

- to appear supportive of the boss in public than to be truly supportive in private

When we feel threatened, we wind up living with masks. To be transparent, we fear, would undermine our position. In the end, we lose the potential for deep relationships with other people. No one really knows us, so no one can really help us. We become isolated, which fuels our insecurity.

When we feel threatened, we
wind up living with masks.

Self-Promotion

I knew of a man who worked for an insecure leader. This leader was asked by his superior to come up with an elaborate instruction manual for a specialty in his field.

But this leader hadn't studied that particular field for years. So he approached this brilliant associate who worked for him and asked him to do the project in his stead.

So, this committed employee spent countless days coming up with a massive, systematic manual. It was beautifully done and quickly acclaimed the resource of choice.

Unfortunately, even though his boss had nothing to do with the creation of the material, he never even indirectly acknowledged that it was done by someone else.

When we feel threatened, we usually don't want to be seen as inferior in any way. As a result, we often won't give credit where credit is due. Instead, we find ourselves twisting situations and conversations so that it seems like, "I did it; I thought of it; I planned it—I deserve the praise." After Saul and the armies of Israel fought the Amalekites, Saul built a statue *for himself*—effectively declaring his own importance in the battle (see 1 Samuel 15:12).

When we feel insecure in our leadership, like Saul, we seek for ways to promote ourselves, even if that means we have to stretch the truth to do so.

Keeping Tight Reins

Leaders who are secure look for opportunities to delegate, not only small tasks, but major responsibilities as well, stepping back and encouraging others to take greater ownership. They recognize people may do things differently than they do, but are happy as long as the work gets done in a timely manner and people are learning and growing. Moses rejoiced when he found out that others were prophesying in the camp and said, "Oh, that all the LORD's people were prophets and that the LORD would put His Spirit upon them!" (Numbers 11:29).

But when we feel insecure in our leadership, we try to keep tight reins on everyone and everything in our reach. We often become micromanagers—telling people exactly what to do and how to do it. If it is not done to a T, it can be taken as insubordination.

We find reasons to do things ourselves instead of delegating responsibilities and encouraging growth. Often we sound godly and perfectly logical in our reasoning, saying things like . . .

- "Why bother them? I am more capable of doing this."

- "They are not as experienced as I am. I can do it better."

- "I can't risk *this* job—I better do it myself."

- "This might be too hard for them."

- "It would be irresponsible to have him do this now. He is not ready."

- "He is too young—people won't listen to him."

- "I don't want him to become discouraged if he can't do it, so I will do it instead."

It may be true that projects need our input or people are not yet ready for greater responsibilities, but we need to be careful. This sort of controlling spirit often marks a leader who feels threatened.

We can start thinking that being the only one who knows how to do something makes us seem more important to our superiors because nothing can go on without us. But it can also be a sinister way of keeping our subordinates "in their place." So instead of empowering others, we tend to say, "You don't need to know that. Just do what I tell you."

We can become leery of approving projects without changing them somehow. Even if it was perfectly done, we feel compelled to "make our mark." If something was allowed to pass without changes, it would "prove" we were not more qualified than the people around us and that we were not essential to the end product.

Whether we realize it or not, we give the impression that nothing is ever good enough without our expertise and input. This sort of direct control is deeply discouraging to those who work with us. People don't have the opportunities to grow and make mistakes, so they remain inexperienced. They can start thinking, "I can never do anything right. Why am I even here?"

Not only do people lose heart, but by making it so no one can function without us, we also become a bottleneck. And soon we can cause slowed growth and development in others.

We naturally try to find security based on external stimuli—praise, affirmation, titles, respect. But stimuli change all the time. They are not something we can control. So instead of looking for security in God, we fight to find stability by trying to control every situation around us.

Clutching at a Title

Being the "in-charge" gives us a sense of stability and control. The more insecure we feel, the more important our title becomes. So when there's a change in our superior's demeanor or even the *hint* of a change coming to our position, all of a sudden we can become nervous and frightened. We worry about being moved, losing favor or being demoted, so we strive even harder to prove ourselves.

True leadership is based on
influence and not on titles.

And when our position seems unstable,
we easily become jealous and suspicious
of any talented individuals around us who
might someday take our place.

Sadly, our title becomes our identity, and
it is hard to imagine life without it. It doesn't
matter if that title is small-group leader, direc-
tor, secretary or Sunday school teacher—our
position and standing become incredibly
important to us.

Although true leadership is based on influence and not on titles, having a position to
call our own seems to provide a sense of security, so we hold onto it with all our strength.

Picking Allies

Imagine a boss has called one of his
employees into his office, wanting to ask an
opinion about another individual he is considering for a promotion.

Now it just so happens that the individual
being asked about works under the first employee. He is a brilliant individual and quite
capable of doing well in the position they are
considering for him.

But during the meeting, the employee

starts to cast doubt on the wisdom of promoting this other individual. He may even sound godly, saying things like, "Scripture says, 'Don't lay a hand on anyone so quickly,' " or "He is a future possibility, but we don't want him to become prideful. Let's not damage him."

The truth of the matter, however, is the employee is afraid of being eclipsed by the other individual and doesn't want him to climb the ladder and take his place. He may not even realize what he is saying or why he is saying it—he simply feels threatened.

It is not hard for us to feel threatened by the advancement of others. It is easy to think, *They must be talented to be promoted so quickly— are they better than me? Are they after my spot? I better be careful!* It was when Saul saw David's successes and growing popularity that he became jealous and frightened (see 1 Samuel 18:6–8, 12, 14–15).

As much as it is up to us, we feel safer surrounding ourselves with people who don't seem like a threat to our position. Unfortunately, that means we are not willing to bring in people who go beyond our abilities.

Sometimes when a yearly review is done, we are able to find extra faults with the ones we feel threatened by. If it is not in their job performance, maybe it will be something vague or imaginary like "bad attitude." We fill the report with more negative comments than good, secretly hoping the other person may get transferred or demoted or may even resign.

Have you ever noticed yourself being more comfortable if the people on staff with you are not as qualified as you are? This can be a symptom of a leader who feels threatened.

Whose Side Are You On?

One of the most damaging results of threatened leadership is found not in the leader himself, but in the people who work with him.

Threatened leaders breed fear into everyone. Co-workers may not be able to identify their insecurity, but they will recognize something is wrong because they breathe insecurity in the air. Insecure leaders cannot provide security for those they lead.

As leaders become unkind and abusive, the people who work with them become like the three monkeys: "I *see* nothing. I *hear* nothing. I *say* nothing." Instead of developing a culture of honesty and humility, people often start playing to the leader's emotions just to survive. To his face, they say, "You are the best!" But in reality, they are just trying to protect themselves. The prevailing attitude becomes, "If you speak the problem, you become the problem."

Because such leaders find it hard to face any sort of criticism, they suspect people are not loyal if they don't speak highly of them. They can think, *Everyone else is saying nice things about me—why aren't they?*

So, like Saul, the man sitting in the boss's chair starts seeing two groups develop: The first is those he thinks of as "on his side"; the other is those he thinks are against him. Those whom he sees as against him are often innocent and sincere; they are not plotting or saying anything bad about him. But to an unstable leader, anyone can become enemy number one. Saul even attacked his son Jonathan because he thought he wasn't "on his side" (see 1 Samuel 20:30–34).

Threatened leaders of today don't have spears like Saul did—they have more "civilized" methods of attack. They can portray submission to authority as a one-way responsibility instead of teaching it in the context of servant-leadership. Disagreement with the leader can be misrepresented as disloyalty to God. Sadly, in the hands of an insecure leader, the Word of God can become twisted into a weapon for his own gain.

Imagine someone you respect were to approach you one day, saying, "I want to help you and be kind to you. Come, sit down, and let me talk to you." And then, opening up the Bible, he uses various well-chosen verses to show you that you are being rebellious. What do you do?

Sadly, this sort of "counseling" happens all too often. It leaves people struggling with guilt, feeling beaten and abused, wondering if they really understand the Lord like they thought they did.

However, if the people who work with the troubled leader understand biblical principles and are sensitive to the Lord, they may recognize the classic story of David and Saul being played out before their eyes. They will probably say to themselves, *I don't want to fight with him, to disrespect him or to gossip about him. But I will pray.* And then, like David, they will often retreat or simply quit, feeling unable to contribute.

Hidden within us all is this dark side that
seeks to maintain the upper hand.

If this sort of abuse goes on too long, eventually there will be no one left who is capable of doing the work. And in the end, the people around the threatened leader become infected with insecurity as well.

We can be doing so well, yet hidden within us all is this dark side that seeks to always maintain the upper hand. It is as Paul said after more than 20 years of preaching, "I am the chief of sinners" (1 Timothy 1:15, paraphrased).

But no matter how dark it seems, this is not the end for us. There remains hope for any individual who is willing to humble his heart and look to God and the answers He provides.

CHAPTER THREE

How Did This Happen?

Imagine somebody goes to see a doctor about a persistent infection he got from cutting his foot. Even though he had washed it, bandaged it and used antibiotics, it continued to fester for many days.

Well, this is interesting, the doctor thinks. *The bacteria are growing much faster than they should be. Why is this?* So he runs some tests. The results show that the patient has high blood sugar due to diabetes. The doctor then explains to his patient how bacteria thrive in the presence of sugar and how just treating the symptoms of the overgrowth won't help his diabetes. "The wound itself is not the main problem," he says. "It is only a symptom of a deeper problem."

The same is true in our leadership. When we deal with the manifestations of striving, fighting and abuse, the real problem is usually more than skin-deep. Like the doctor, we have to ask, what is causing this? How do we become threatened leaders? What are the reasons?

An Insecure World

Looking to the world around us can give us some clues. People often feel insecure in their leadership because they lead based on faulty concepts.

> Without us even knowing, we are drawn to think in worldly terms of what it means to be successful in leadership.

The vast majority of books on leadership contain stories, comparisons and instructions from politicians, athletes and others who are successful according to the world's standards. And so, without us even knowing, we are drawn to think in worldly terms of what it means to be successful in leadership.

There is the business model, which teaches us about return on investment, ROI. Here we continually ask the question, "What do I get out of it?" Profit motivates every action—position, recognition, money or other benefits.

Then you have the political world. Politicians often become crowd-pleasers, using every means possible to get the majority of voters on their side. The unspoken drive is to gain power and influence.

Consider the sports model—people can devote their lives to intense, disciplined training, seeking to be the best, looking forward to the time they will be recognized for their efforts and hear the crowds cheering their name. Christian leaders who have this mindset are disciplined and work hard to accomplish their goals. Their efforts may appear to be for spiritual reasons, but it often ends up being for self-glory.

Gene Edwards, author of *A Tale of Three Kings*, wrote,

> Many pray for the power of God. More every year. Those prayers sound powerful, sincere, godly, and without ulterior motive. Hidden under such prayer and fervor, however, are ambition, a craving for fame, the desire to be considered a spiritual giant. The person who prays such a prayer may not even know it, but dark motives and desires are in his heart.[1]

Unfortunately, people who lead based on these worldly models are predisposed to feeling unsettled in their leadership. They always have to watch out for others who are coming up the ranks, because everything is a competition. Newcomers are seen as threats, not blessings.

Family Background

People often see others through the coloring of their upbringing, which can cause them to become insecure in their leadership.

It is easy to find a threat around every corner when that's what you're accustomed to finding.

Leaders who come from abusive or domineering homes are prone to perceiving others as threats. Even if the leader hated such tyranny in his past, he can sometimes revert to such behavior with his subordinates. This is especially true with co-workers who don't immediately fall in line with everything the leader wants to do.

Leaders who have grown up in environments where everything is a competition and a fight for survival often think that everyone is out to get them and anyone with a different opinion is a danger.

It is easy to find a threat around every corner when that's what you're accustomed to finding.

Fear

It is hard to be insecure in our leadership without being afraid of something. And whether what we fear is real or imaginary, the effects are devastating.

From the time we are young, it seems we are always afraid of something. It is natural, like breathing. We fear both the known and the unknown. And even though studies show most things we fear seldom happen, we continue to be afraid.

Job was a man who seemed to have everything going for him. He had respect, wealth, healthy children and a multitude of servants. His influence stretched far and wide, and he was even called the greatest of the men of the East (see Job 1:1–3).

But even when everything was going well for him, Job was afraid. Soon all that he had was destroyed. And after sitting in ashes, not speaking for seven days, Job makes a very revealing statement: "The thing I greatly *feared* has come upon me" (see Job 2:13; 3:25, *emphasis mine*).

That means, when all his cattle were safe, he feared they would be taken. When his children were healthy and secure, he feared they would perish. In fact, he was so concerned that they might sin unintentionally that he regularly offered sacrifices on their behalf, as a preventative measure to be sure they were in good standing with God (see Job 1:5).

It is often when things are going especially well that we start to fear it going away. We tend to think, *All good things must come to an end* and *What goes up must come down.* Unfortunately, that theory means the higher we are and the more we are given, the more we have to worry about losing. And as leaders, the Lord has given us much—authority, status, respect, finances and people who look up to us. It is very easy for fearful thoughts to sneak in—thoughts that maybe everything will fail or fall apart.

It is often when things are going especially
well that we start to fear it going away.

I know of several able leaders who made a shipwreck of their lives by giving in to fear about the financial security of their future. Many others were destroyed because they gave into fear that people were out to get them or that they might be sent somewhere they did not want to go.

Saul was terrified of what might happen to him if David continued gaining popularity, and he strove to prevent David's success. But in the end, it was Saul who lost out on every-thing.

Instead of taking responsibility for the negative thoughts of fear, there are times for all of us that we allow these fears to control us. And when we do that, we are stepping into the realm of uncertainty and instability.

Lack of Submission

Imagine a soldier has decided not to submit to his commanding officer by go-ing somewhere he was not directed to go. When enemy fire comes, the commander will not know someone is in danger because he expects his soldiers to be where he told them to be. Standing alone, such a soldier will feel very insecure very quickly.

When someone is not sure the decisions they make are approved by their authority, their security is uncertain. There were several times Saul didn't do what he had been told, such as when he offered a sacrifice he was not authorized to offer (see 1 Samuel 13:8–14) and when he spared Agag and his cattle when he was supposed to destroy them (see 1 Samuel 15:1–9). Saul lived a life of inde-pendence and disobedience, which fueled his insecurity.

Often when we are first put in positions of leadership, we work hard to keep in touch with our authorities. We share our thoughts and plans, and if we need help or don't understand something, we are quick to ask for assistance. It's not a matter of getting permission for everything; it's more just keeping our superiors informed.

Unresolved sins can be like rust,
eating us away on the inside.

But the longer people are in leadership, the more likely they are to fall into a deadly trap. They start to think, *I've been doing this now for so many years, and I have succeeded in all these ways. Why do I still have to check with my leaders all the time and keep telling them what is going on?* They can even become reluctant about bringing things up for approval or direction, fearing their leader will tell them something they don't want to hear.

Eventually a crisis occurs or an issue comes up that they don't know how to handle—it happens to all of us. Leaders who have open relationships with their authorities can go to them for help. But leaders who are in the habit of keeping their lips sealed and acting independently feel compelled to face these problems on their own. In reality, there are plenty of people willing to support them, but these leaders made the choice to stand unprotected and alone.

Unresolved Guilt

Unresolved sin and guilt is another reason for insecurity.

So often the Enemy gets ahold of somebody's mind, saying, "Wow, what you did was really bad. If they find out, they are going to . . ." and then he insinuates all sorts of terrible things based on what we fear most.

Soon we start to think, *When they find out, they're going to sack me! I don't want to bring it up.*

Please know—we all fail. We all make mistakes. But when we are not willing to repent and walk in the light, the unresolved sins can be like rust, eating us away on the inside.

When our hearts aren't right it's like standing on sand—it will crumble underneath us.

Sense of Inadequacy

It is not uncommon for leaders to live with a sense of inadequacy, especially in the face of the vastness of the Lord's kingdom work.

Imagine there is a young man whom God has called to work with a ministry. Despite his apparent lack of experience, the leadership feels it is the Lord's will to promote him.

Soon he is placed in a position of authority over a department. But everyone in that department is older and much more experienced than he is. It is hard to imagine this man doesn't feel at least a little bit inadequate for the task before him.

When God approached Moses and told him to lead Israel out of Egypt, Moses said, "Please find somebody else; I can't even talk" (Exodus 4:10–13, paraphrased). Jeremiah told God, "I cannot speak: for I am a child" (Jeremiah 1:6, KJV). The theologian Charles Spurgeon once said, "Who was I that I should continue to lead so great a multitude?"[2]

This sense of inadequacy can drive people to the Lord in dependence upon Him, or it can be a reason for them to feel anxious and uncertain in their position.

Lack of Discipline

Sometimes leaders lose security when they aren't disciplined enough to keep up with information, technology and methodology they need to function in their role.

Consider the medical field. In order to stay on top in their profession, doctors and nurses must be perpetual students. A constant influx of newer diagnostic techniques, new medications and research findings demands they continue to learn.

Similarly, anyone who doesn't grow will quickly become incapable of doing their job efficiently. Without discipline, we naturally feel inadequate and, ultimately, threatened by others who are capable of doing things we have not been disciplined enough to learn.

Criticism

Anyone who takes up the mantle of leadership will face opposition and criticism. Moses, Paul, David and Jesus Himself all faced criticism. *No one is above being criticized.*

Despite how common it is, it is one of the reasons why we can feel threatened in our leadership.

When all we hear is how we are failing and doing things wrong all the time, it can begin to wear us down. We start thinking, *Maybe I really* am *a failure. I thought I was doing the right thing, but it looks like it turned out all wrong. I just don't know what to do.*

Criticism *can* be an opportunity for growth, even if it was told with the intent to hurt. But facing criticism often makes us defensive. We naturally want to prove somehow, both to our leaders and to those around us, that what people say about us is not true. We become concerned about maintaining our image and trying to clear our name. Criticism can cause us to focus on ourselves instead of focusing on God's sovereignty, leading us to feel overwhelmed by the waves of uncertainty around us.

Damaging Influences

Leaders can become threatened when they allow the wrong influences in their lives.

Imagine someone you know comes to you one day saying, "You are my friend. We've known each other for years. Let's have a cup of tea."

You sit down together in a café, and the waiter brings you your drinks. But right before you drink your tea, your friend says, "Oh, wait a minute."

And he takes out a dark little bottle from the recesses of his coat. While you are watching, he takes off the cap, pours a little bit into your tea and stirs it in.

Naturally you ask him, "What is this?"

"Oh," he says, "it is something quite nice for your health."

Then he puts the bottle down on the table. You see the picture of a skull and crossbones on the label. Underneath it, in screaming-red capital letters, it reads: "Poison: One Drop Can Kill an Elephant."

Question: Will you drink what he offers you?

Sadly, too often we take in something just as toxic—not in our beverages, but in our conversations.

Who we listen to and where we get our information from are critically important. Often leaders are only told what others *think* they want to hear, even if it is just speculation.

Who we listen to and where we get our information from are critically important.

There are always going to be people who bring evil reports and gossip. They may even do it in an effort to earn our favor and get on our side.

When we choose to listen to gossip, it can take root in our hearts. And then we begin believing the stories we hear, whether consciously or subconsciously.

Soon we start to think that the boss is favoring another person or someone is not really loyal to us. Our future feels uncertain. Then sadly, when we start behaving as though these statements are true, it breeds more fear and insecurity.

Not only that, we must be aware of people praising us and saying wonderful things about us all the time. In Luke 6:26,

Jesus said, "Woe to you when all men speak well of you." Flattery actually kills. Saint Augustine, an early church father, said it this way, "The adversary of our true blessedness layeth hard at us, every where spreading his snares of 'well-done, well-done.' "[3]

> It may sound like gossipers and
> flatterers care about you, but
> hidden in that "care" is poison.

Sometimes people will learn what to say to twist a leader's thoughts to their own ends. On the surface, it may sound like gossipers and flatterers care about you and want to help you, but hidden in that "care" is tremendously destructive poison.

Trusting in Self

One of the most devastating reasons for leaders to feel threatened is because they begin to trust in their own strength and abilities instead of trusting in the Lord alone.

Over time it happens—we learn, we grow and we begin to rely on our past experiences and our skills instead of relying on the Lord. Although we wouldn't say it outright, we begin thinking, *I am somebody now. Why fast and pray to find out what God is saying? I can figure it out.*

Imagine with me that you have an aboveground water tower, one that holds more than 5 million liters. If the tank depends solely on what it already has stored to supply water for all the people who live around it, it will quickly run dry. However, the water tank depends on more than its own supply. It depends on the vast supply of water under the ground.

In the same way, when we as leaders depend on ourselves, we are limited to our own current resources. Instead of putting our faith in God and tapping into a much greater supply of help, strength, energy, motivation and encouragement, we will find ourselves quickly running out of what we have, unable to meet the needs and the expectations on us.

It says in the Scripture, "Cursed is the man who trusts in man and makes flesh his strength, whose heart departs from the LORD" (Jeremiah 17:5). What a statement. Cursed be that individual, that man, that woman, who began so well, trusting God without any pride or arrogance, but now has come to the place of trusting in their own strength and ability.

When a leader does not have the inner godliness to meet the needs of the people around him, God may raise up someone like David to be the answer for the people. And it is natural for the self-reliant leader to feel angry, troubled and jealous when he sees them meeting needs he cannot meet.

Fellowship with the Lord

No matter what position of authority God gives you, there is one thing that guarantees insecurity in your leadership. It is not other people, it is not others' misbehavior, it is not lack of money, it is not lack of recognition, it is not lack of degrees, it is not lack of opportunity—it is a broken relationship with the Living God. Without Him, you *will* be insecure.

CHAPTER FOUR

Forging Another Way

We've seen what threatened leadership looks like and the environment it creates. We walked through the reasons for it. And now, what must you and I do to avoid these kinds of pitfalls?

What we need to know is that true security will never come through how many people are following us, through our titles, connections, possessions or our skills. Anything we try to figure out by our own deductions becomes very horizontal and humanistic. Following the Lord and His principles is at the root of becoming stable and secure leaders. And as Thomas à Kempis said, "Disregard outward appearances and diligently . . . cultivate such things as foster amendment of life and fervour of soul, rather than . . . cultivate those qualities that seem most popular."[1] We need to begin to think with a new paradigm and forge another way.

Be Your Own Judge

Anyone who wants to survive in leadership, with all the struggles and temptations, must be their own judge. Why? Especially as a leader, you may find that few people will say anything bad about you to your face. It may be helpful for you to seek out two or three people who can share with you honestly when they see problems in your attitude and actions.

But ultimately, you must be responsible to judge yourself. First Corinthians 11:28–31 encourages us to judge and examine ourselves. If you sense that there is some kind of alienation in you toward other people or from other people and you find yourself becoming critical toward others, you need to stop and ask yourself the question: *What is happening? Why am I thinking like this?*

You'll be surprised—most of the time the problem is within you. It's *only then* that we can begin to change.

The first thing we need to do is to be willing to see our need for change. Refrain from the natural tendency to justify your thoughts and your actions. Be willing to let truth speak without hindrance. However painful it might be, judge yourself truthfully.

Safe with God

No one can be a threat to your character and who you really are. No matter what is happening, where we are sent or what people say, our security rests in our right relationship with God and with man.

We will be secure when we
have nothing to hide.

So it's critical that we maintain honest relationships with co-laborers and superiors, even if that means admitting failure and asking for forgiveness. Be willing to be transparent. We will be secure when we have nothing to hide. Even our enemies may come around when we make decisions based on integrity.

When we find that we are troubled, emotionally disturbed or afraid, we must *go back to God*. When the future looks grim, we need to focus on His faithfulness and trust in His promises, promises like: "My God shall supply all your need according to His riches in glory by Christ Jesus" (Philippians 4:19).

God will never leave us, He will never forsake us and we will never be helpless (see Matthew 28:20; Psalm 46:1). He will provide for our needs and give us the grace to do all that He asks of us (see Philippians 2:13).

God will never leave us, He will never forsake us and we will never be helpless.

Over the years, I have seen many people who forgot God's promises and destroyed their lives as they sought security in finances and material things instead. It happened to many people in the Bible.

Look at Gehazi. What potential that man had! But he went after money and lost everything (see 2 Kings 5:19–27). Judas betrayed the Lord Jesus for a bag of silver and wound up losing his life (see Matthew 26:14–16, 27:4–5). All of Solomon's wealth, power and influence brought him no satisfaction (see Ecclesiastes 2:1–11). Our security will *never* come from a better position, having more money, marrying someone or having a bigger following.

I testify to you, over these decades of walking with my Lord, the only times I have lost peace, stability and time were when I used my own logic to interpret life and make my choices. I'm sad for those seasons.

However, when I had no argument and just followed the Lord and trusted Him, I found life was beautiful, and there was such peace.

Cultivating a Safe Environment

Written nearly 600 years ago, Thomas à Kempis's words are for us today:

> God has so ordained it, that we should learn to bear one another's burdens, for there is no one who has not some defect, no one without some burden, no man independent of others, no one wise enough of himself; but we ought to bear with one another, comfort one another, help, instruct, and advise one another.[2]

We need each other. If we are not a team, we *will* burn out. If we try to make it all happen on our own, we will fail. We *need* one another.

In Acts 2:14 (NIV) we read, "Then Peter stood up with the Eleven . . . " It was not Peter standing alone, but Peter standing together with the apostles as one unit. Everything God does is in unity. He is the Trinity. It is all three persons in the Trinity being one that make up the godhead. It is by working together with mankind that God brings about His purposes. If there were any being who could do something without anyone, it is God. Yet He still chose to work with us to build His kingdom.

Genuine proof that someone is led by the Holy Spirit is that they don't have the attitude, "I am the most important one," but instead, "I am one among all." It is by God's grace that we are in the positions that God has given us. That person sitting across from us may be far more brilliant than us, and they very well may have something more important to say. Don't be threatened by them, but instead see their brilliance as your team being strengthened. Listen to what they have to say.

We give others security when we are secure without having to be the best. And they give us moral authority when they see we are not moved by who is better.

Don't necessarily view disagreements as disloyalty or insubordination. In such times, guard your heart from seeking to get your own way, and value others' opinions. Be open to change and seek the best solution, not just your own thought. Criticism can be constructive, even if it was intended to hurt. Don't just reject it outright when people criticize you, but try to find the truth in it, even if it is only five percent of what they said.

Remember Jesus' words to Peter, "Feed My

sheep" (John 21:17). God didn't bring these people under your care just to "get the job done," but also so they could grow into His likeness.

We give others security when we are
secure without having to be the best.

Actively seek to cultivate their skills and their ambition to serve God. Follow Christ's example of how He led and trained His disciples. Begin by simply explaining what you expect and giving them the opportunity to ask questions. Then show them how to do it by the things that practically come up. The next step is to give them the opportunity to do it as you watch on. Give them credit for what they have done. Then give them opportunity to do it on their own. If there is a deficiency, come alongside them and help them see how to improve.

Ask yourself questions like: *How can I inspire them to rise to their full potential? How can I train them to understand my thinking and do this without me in the future?* Seek also to encourage their godliness, humility and walk with God.

As leaders, God has given us a tremendous assignment to recognize those whom the

Lord is calling into positions of leadership. Ask God to help you understand His appointing for them. Give them opportunities to learn, grow and fail, and empower them to go forward. Anticipate and even look forward to the day that, with the proper training and input, you can hand your position over to them.

The ultimate proof of our leadership is the way we enabled others to go far beyond us.

I am still learning to apply some of these principles too. But if we truly want to make a difference for the generation to come, we must lead and empower others based on the future—5, 10, 20, 50 years from now. The ultimate proof of our leadership is not only what *we* have done, but also the way we enabled others to go far beyond us.

An Aerial View

Everything looks different when you are in an airplane. What seems big on the ground can look very small when you have a higher perspective. Life on earth is so short. It is essential that we don't become distracted by focusing on the here and now instead of the much bigger picture.

The writer of Psalm 73 was a leader in

God's work. He saw those who didn't follow God's ways, yet they seemed to get everything (see Psalm 73:3, 12). We can just imagine they must have had their mansions, bank accounts, cars—the list goes on. He was envious and basically says to himself, *I have nothing! I've been faithful, but for what?! Why don't I have all these things? What have I done with my life?* (see Psalm 73:13–14).

Then he talked to God about it, and God opened his eyes. He began to see things from a different perspective. And he responds, essentially saying, "Oh my God! I didn't realize that they are standing on slippery ground. Everything is going to get burned up. Their position, power, everything—it has no meaning. It is all for such a short time" (see Psalm 73:16–19).

And in the end he concludes, "It is good for me to draw near to God" (Psalm 73:28).

Read through Ecclesiastes, and it will add some soberness to your thinking. Nothing is permanent here.

We are all smart people. But keep in mind that a day is coming when every intention and thought of our hearts shall be revealed and judged. Don't focus your life around fleeting, temporal things instead of the One who is eternal.

Ecclesiastes concludes by saying: "Fear God, and keep his commandments: for this is the whole duty of man. For God shall bring every work into judgment, with every secret thing, whether it be good, or whether it be evil" (Ecclesiastes 12:13–14, KJV).

Live with the fear of God in view of that Day of Judgment. We can try to fool each other by projecting something we are not, but God sees and He knows. One day we all will stand before His throne and hear what God has to say about how we led our lives. This is a sobering reality.

We have been given much, especially as leaders, and we will have much to give an account for. We also will give an account for the people He asked us to lead (see Hebrews 13:17). As Thomas à Kempis said, "The more you know and understand, the heavier will be your judgment, unless, in consequence of your greater knowledge, your life is a more holy one."[3] Because God is the One who put us where we are, our aim should be to please Him.

As leaders and as children of God, the only honor and praise we should seek is that which comes from the Lord in the end.

Appointed by God

God is sovereign, and we can trust Him. He is the One who appointed us to our leadership position, according to Romans 13:1–2.

So when our popularity begins to wane, when our position seems to be in flux or when we feel inadequate for the task at hand, we have nothing to worry about. It is all in the Lord's hands.

Consider John the Baptist. He was in the public eye long before Christ; he had numerous disciples and a lot of public attention. But soon people started going to Jesus more than they were going to John. So one day some of John's people brought this to his attention, essentially saying, "Master, we've got a problem. Jesus is getting the big crowds now. You are losing your popularity" (see John 3:26).

But John basically says, "You don't understand. We can't receive anything unless it has come from God. I'm really happy that Jesus is receiving all this attention. Don't you remember? I came to promote Him. This was the role I was given to play. I'm not threatened; I'm so content" (see John 3:28–30).

John the Baptist *knew* that God was the One who placed him where he was, and this knowledge gave him security, regardless of the position and title he held. Even when John's disciples joined Jesus, John was glad because he understood the larger picture (see John 1:35–37).

Even when we feel overwhelmed in our position, we can rest in the Lord. When we are a leader, it is very common for us to face new challenges and crises. We may not weep on the outside, but inside often we are trembling and thinking, *I don't know if I can do this!*

We cannot afford to evaluate situations based only on ourselves—we must make conclusions based on God.

Whether you think you are qualified or not, remember, it was God who placed you in this position of responsibility. Therefore, you can be sure that God will give you the ability you need to do it.

It is true that we must be constant, disciplined learners, but at the same time, we cannot afford to evaluate situations based only on ourselves—we must make conclusions based on God. That's what David did when faced with the giant. He told Goliath, "You may look big, but I am not coming in my name; I am coming in the name of a God who makes me able" (1 Samuel 17:45, paraphrased). Jonathan Edwards, a respected theologian from the 1700s, said,

> A truly humble man . . . is sensible of his natural distance from God; of his dependence on him; of the insufficiency of his own power and wisdom, and that it

is by God's power that he is upheld and
provided for, and that he needs God's
wisdom to lead and guide him, and his
might to enable him to do what he ought
to do for him.[4]

There will always be people who might
do your job better than you. But God didn't
call them to fill the position you are in. He
called *you*, and no one can harm you.

Know that He will protect you and continue to stand by you if you remain humble
and your heart is with the Lord.

Our Father

Jesus told a remarkable parable about two
brothers. We find it in the Gospel of Luke
15:11–32.

The younger brother takes all the money
he can and runs off, lives a bad life and wastes
everything. Then he repents and goes home.

His father is loving and gracious to him.
Soon the younger brother is in the house
having the time of his life—the best mutton
curry and the best mango and the best ice
cream. But somebody is missing from the
dining table—it's the older brother.

The father is so happy, but the older son is
seething, refusing to go inside and celebrate.
He snaps at his father and basically says, "I've
been living in this house all these years, and

I've served you like a slave! I never wasted your money! I built this! I did that! I did everything you said!

"And you never gave me a feast! But you give one to this worthless, no-good son of yours who wasted all your money! I don't want to come inside" (Luke 15:28–30, paraphrased).

And the father basically replies, "My son, my son. All of these things are yours! You can have beef-fry, mutton-curry every morning, day and night. It's all yours! Whoever told you it's not yours?" (see Luke 15:31).

Question: How do you explain this?

Even when the younger son was a rebel, his heart was knit with the affection of his father. So when everything was gone, he said to himself, *I can go to my father.*

But for the older son, it was different. Even when everything was provided, he could not get inside the house. His relationship with his father was not one of father and son; rather, it was an employer and his employee. He was working for wages: respect, recognition and understanding.

Even though he had all the possibilities as the eldest son, his heart was not in a loving relationship with his father. In Christianity and Christian leadership, this same thing can happen. You are a great leader, and you have so much to do. But in the end you can come to the place in which you are doing all the work for money, recognition, reputation, honor or whatever else. It's all about what *you* get, not because of the affection of the Father who sees you in secret.

Spiritual realities are always a mystery. When God deals with us, deep down in our hearts, there is a sense that *we know* something happened. Everything changed for me when I realized I am not a mission leader, I am not a politician, but I am a father—a father to those the Lord has given me.

When we realize that God is *our* Father and we are safe in His hands *and* that we are to be a father to those He has given us—everything changes.

It's no longer so hard to know we are safe.

CHAPTER FIVE

Living with Threatened Leaders

In the very early years of my life serving God, I had a leader over me who seemed to view me as a potential threat to his position. Life became difficult for many years.

Maybe as you've been reading this booklet, you've recognized that someone in your life might feel threatened *by you*. We can never know for certain what is in someone's heart. But if you think that's the case, there are some principles that are helpful for you to know and do in relating to this leader.

- *Don't take revenge* or attempt to take matters into your own hands. Trust God.

- *Learn obedience through suffering.* Difficult

seasons are a tool God uses to prepare
you for greater purpose and blessing in
your life.

- *Ask yourself* if there is something you are
doing or not doing, saying or not saying,
which causes people to feel threatened
by you. Make any necessary changes.

- *Read the Word.* Learn from the examples
of people who lived under threatened
leaders, like David and Jonathan who
lived under Saul.

- *Live in submission* to your authority. I
recommend you read my book *Touching
Godliness*.[1]

- *Pray* specifically for God to help that
leader. Pray for any specific situation,
struggle or problem that you know is affecting him, his actions and behavior.

- *Go* to the person in humility and love
and share with him your concerns, if the
Lord leads you to do so. Share with him
in humility and leave the "back door"
open. Don't be hasty—give God time to
work in his heart.

- *Read* Chapter 10 of *Touching Godliness*,
"When Our Authorities Go Wrong."

There are some practical guides you will find helpful.[2]

- *Embrace humility.* Avoid seeking attention and praise for what you do. Be a servant who seeks to please the Lord, remembering that this is His work. Take courage in Saint Francis's words:

"O Divine Master, grant that I may not so much seek to be consoled, as to console; to be understood, as to understand; to be loved, as to love; for it is in giving that we receive, it is in pardoning that we are pardoned, and it is in dying that we are born to eternal life."[3]

CHAPTER SIX

Things to Remember

No matter who we are, where we come from or how long we have been on the journey, we all need to be reminded.

Finding our security in Christ is not an instantaneous event. Rather, it is a continuous, gradual, growing process.

Here is a checklist to keep at hand to remember these important principles in being a leader who promotes a secure environment and prepares leaders for the years ahead. The best is yet to come.

- Constantly judge yourself and your motives.

- Seek counsel.

- Find truth in criticism.

- Remember what counts—not your position, but your character.

- Learn to be vulnerable.

- Remember the promises of God:

  "For I know the thoughts that I think toward you, says the LORD, thoughts of peace and not of evil, to give you a future and a hope" (Jeremiah 29:11).

  "For there is no authority except from God, and the authorities that exist are appointed by God" (Romans 13:1).

  "I will never leave you nor forsake you" (Hebrews 13:5).

  "I have been young, and now am old; yet I have not seen the righteous forsaken, nor his descendants begging bread" (Psalm 37:25).

- Trust in God.

- Learn the meaning of servant-leadership.

- Be a team player.

- Acknowledge others.

- Be a constant learner.

- Continue growing through discipline and study.

- Remember that life is short.

- Think future—10, 20, 50, 100 years from now.

- Know you are secure as long as you walk with God.

Prayer

Father, thank You for the joy of knowing You and the instruction that we receive from Your Word.

Sometimes, Lord, we are so occupied with the present world that we miss the future. Please open our eyes so we become more concerned about You and Your kingdom than about the little things that occupy our attention.

Help us, we pray, as leaders, to find ways to empower people, to trust them and give them freedom, with guidance and coaching at the right time.

We are weak, but You are strong. We fail so often, but Lord, You are gracious to us and keep us going. So we humbly ask You to help us guard our hearts and minds and walk closely to You, knowing that in the end, You are the only One who really matters.

Forgive us our foolishness and our forgetfulness.
May we trust You with our lives and our re-
sponsibilities and travel with You to the end.
Thank You for answering our prayers. In
Jesus' name, Amen.

Notes

Front Matter

[1] C.S. Lewis, *Mere Christianity* (New York, NY: Macmillan, 1943), p. 190.

Chapter 1

[1] Definition taken from *Merriam-Webster.com*. 2011. (http://www.merriam-webster.com/dictionary/insecure). (Accessed May 23, 2012).

[2] Definition taken from *Merriam-Webster.com*. 2011. (http://www.merriam-webster.com/dictionary/threatened). (Accessed May 23, 2012).

Chapter 3

[1] Gene Edwards, *A Tale of Three Kings* (Newnan, GA: SeedSowers, 1980), pp. 40–41.

[2] Charles Spurgeon, *C.H. Spurgeon's Autobiography, Volume 1* (London, England: Passmore and Alabaster, 1899), p. 362.

[3] Saint Augustine, *The Confessions of S. Augustine* (Oxford, 1853), p. 216.

Chapter 4

[1] Thomas à Kempis, *The Imitation of Christ*, ed. Read How You Want Pty Ltd (Sydney, Australia: Objective Systems Pty Ltd, 2006), p. 239.

[2] Thomas à Kempis, *Of the Imitation of Christ*, ed. and trans. W.H. Hutchings (Waterloo Place, London: Rivingtons, 1881), p. 25.

[3] *Ibid.*, p. 3.

[4] Jonathan Edwards, *Christian Love and It's [sic] Fruit* (La Vergne, TN: Lightning Source, 2001), p. 65.

Chapter 5

[1] K.P. Yohannan, *Touching Godliness* (Carrollton, TX: GFA Books, 2011).

[2] *Ibid.*, pp. 197–214.

[3] Lawrence Cunningham, *Francis of Assisi: Performing the Gospel Life* (Grand Rapids, MI: Wm. B. Eerdmans, 2004), p. 146.

Also by K.P. Yohannan

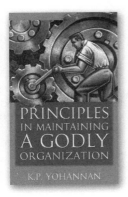

Principles in Maintaining a Godly Organization

Remember the "good old days" in your ministry? This booklet provides a biblical basis for maintaining that vibrancy and commitment that accompany any new move of God. (48 pages)

Revolution in World Missions

Step into the story of missionary statesman K.P. Yohannan and experience the world through his eyes. You will hang on every word—from the villages of India to the shores of Europe and North America. Watch out: His passion is contagious! (240 pages)

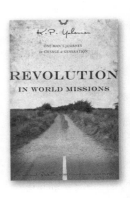

Travel to the mission field— for a few hours

Even though you don't live with the millions of people in South Asia or experience their unique cultures and struggles, you can intercede for them!

By joining in **Gospel for Asia's live-streaming prayer meetings**, you can step inside their world through stories, photos and videos. You might even change, too. Here's what other people said about the prayer meetings:

"I don't think I ever come away with a dry eye from these prayer meetings. It is so encouraging to me to see the Lord working so mightily in so many ways in the world."
—Sheri

"It is so good and helpful to hear of the needs and to sense God's Spirit at work. It helps me to pray more earnestly and to be a part of what God is doing in your ministry."
—Timothy

"Praise Jesus! I love having a team to pray with." —Mia

Pray with us!
Go to **www.gfa.org/pray** for schedules and to participate in the streamed prayer meetings.